The Book of the
CORONATION PACIFICS
A Photographic Accompaniment: 1

By
Ian Sixsmith

IRWELL PRESS Ltd.

Cover photographs: 46248 CITY OF LEEDS
at Camden shed on 7 August 1963 (Peter
Groom). 46245 CITY OF LONDON (the most
photographed Coronation by far in the last
few years, it would seem) is at the other
end of the line, leaving Glasgow Central
with the up Caledonian, 8 April 1958 (James
Stevenson, courtesy Hamish Stevenson).

First published in the United Kingdom in 2005
by Irwell Press Limited, 59A, High Street, Clophill,
Bedfordshire MK45 4BE
Printed by Newnorth, Bedford

The engine and the train it was intended for. New 'streamliner' 6220 CORONATION 'storms through the Northern Fells' (as the publicity usually put it – the location is actually Elvanfoot, on the climb to Beattock) with the up Coronation Scot in the early days of the service.

Contemporary postcard to celebrate the new transport wonder: CORONATION hurtles through an atmospheric evening at Bourne End with the Coronation Scot. The train did not normally carry a reporting number so it is to be suspected (especially as an official photographer was there) that this is the pre-launch 'special'.

THE "CORONATION SCOT" PASSING THROUGH
BOURNE END.

A PHOTOGRAPH FROM "THE TIMES

CORONATION about to breast the summit of Camden Bank with the down working of the new train, before passing Camden shed.

THE BOOK OF THE CORONATION PACIFICS
A Pictorial Accompaniment: 1
Notes by Ian Sixsmith

Picture This

The last seven years has seen the Irwell Press 'Book Of' series of locomotive studies blossom into a sought-after library covering more and more of the principal express classes. Some have been reprinted while others are out of print; others remain to be reprinted. Beginning in 1997 the sequence has been:

The Book of the BR Standards
The Book of the Coronation Pacifics
The Book of the Royal Scots
The Book of the Merchant Navy Pacifics
The Book of the Jubilee 4-6-0s
The Book of the West Country/Battle of Britain Pacifics
The Book of the Princess Royal Pacifics
The Book of the Patriot 4-6-0s
The Book of the BR Standards: 2
The Book of the A3 Pacifics
The Book of the Britannias

Most recently, there has been *The Book of the Britannias: A Photographic Accompaniment*, its purpose to serve up a wider range of photographs for that particularly popular class. Cue a suitable 'Accompaniment' for each of the locomotive classes in the series and this volume, for the Stanier Coronations (or Princess Coronations, Duchesses, 'semis' 'Big Lizzies', 'big 'uns', call them what you will) is the second effort so far. It accompanies, supplements and complements the second 'Book Of', *The Book of the Coronation Pacifics*, first published in 1998, subsequently reprinted twice and long out of print – until now. The third 'Accompaniment' another slender volume dedicated to the Coronation Pacifics comes next…

****

I would like to thank Eric Youldon, Barry Hoper, Richard Derry, Allan Baker, Peter Rowledge, John Corkill, Bryan Wilson, Graham Onley and Martin Smith in compiling this pictorial.

In Brief

Stanier's range of standard locomotives has come to personify the LMS, and the thinking and practice that suffused it carried over into the Standard locomotives of British Railways. So it said in *The Book of the Coronation Pacifics*. We won't repeat any sort of detail history here, for this is a Photographic Accompaniment, and (to use a modern cliché) it does just what it says on the tin. Stanier was appointed from 1 January 1932, in circumstances that are well known and well recorded. LMS locomotive policy lay largely in ruins – just ask Sir Harold Hartley of the LMS: *'Stanier was the man to get our locomotive programme straightened out. The number of different types we had inherited was appalling...'*

A revolution was necessary (indeed expected) and Stanier duly made his way from Swindon and the GWR with loins thoroughly girded. His 'mighty re-stocking' (to use H.A.V. Bulleid's phrase) was about to begin. The taper boiler version of the Hughes 2-6-0, in response to a request from the Operating people for 'more Crabs' signalled The Way Forward but next it had to be the newest and biggest express passenger locomotive of the age. A great Pacific duly emerged. It had four cylinders ('because he was used to it', says Bulleid) but these, the Princess Royals, were only essays in the craft and amounted to just thirteen, including the famous 'Turbomotive'. They were built in two batches; 6200 appeared in July 1933 and 6212 in October 1935.

Batch after Batch

The Book of the Coronation Pacifics

Typical railway publicity of the period, 6229 DUCHESS OF HAMILTON in primer at Crewe Works in 1938. LION had been built a hundred years before and once the Duchess was complete the two were filmed together on the North Wales main line, to wring some more footage for the PR people. Does the film still exist? In the days when the railway could do such things the entire four tracks of the main line between Llandudno Junction and Colwyn Bay were closed so that 6220 with the Coronation Scot could be filmed running abreast of the 1911 Coronation train hauled by George V No.25348, and the Liverpool & Manchester Railway replica train hauled by LION. If this were not enough, on the fourth line was 4-4-0 No.695 with a brake van and something called a scenery truck, 'overtaking or running parallel with the trains as required'.

ALLOCATION UPDATE

The Book of the Coronation Pacifics was the first of its kind and adhered strictly to the information as given in the LMS/BR Engine Record Cards. As is well known, the assiduous recording of steam locomotive mileages and other items fell out of use once it was clear the engines were doomed, from about 1960. With the benefit of hindsight, however, it is clear that the allocations at least, should have been brought up to date. So, using contemporary references, **Graham Onley** has completed the allocations given in *The Book of the Coronation Pacifics*, in the cases where they they do not run 'fully to term' thus:

46220 Polmadie 15/5/43, Crewe North 6/58, Carlisle Upperby 2/61.

46221 Crewe North 1/10/60, Carlisle Upperby 2/61, Carlisle Kingmoor 3/61. Carlisle Upperby 7/4/62.

46224 *reasonable to assume* initial 1939 allocation Camden, then Polmadie 30/12/39 to withdrawal.

46226 Carlisle <u>Upperby</u> 5/3/55, Crewe North 29/9/56, Carlisle Upperby 20/10/56. Carlisle Kingmoor 3/61.

46228 Carlisle Upperby 20/6/59, Crewe North 6/59.

46229 Crewe North 1/10/49, Camden 6/52, Crewe North 9/60, Edge Hill 3/61.

46234 the 'official' entries dated 7 and 21/11/59 make clear that withdrawal came from Carlisle Upperby; did the clerk 'nod off' or something?

46236 Carlisle Upperby 14/6/58, Edge Hill 1/61, Carlisle Upperby 2/61, Carlisle Kingmoor 3/11/62.

46237 Carlisle Upperby 14/6/58, Carlisle Kingmoor 3/61, Carlisle Upperby 7/4/62.

46239 Camden 11/11/44, Holyhead 24/8/63, Willesden 9/63, Crewe North 8/64.

46240 Willesden 7/9/63, Crewe North 8/64.

46241 Crewe North 20/9/58, Edge Hill 3/61.

46243 Camden 11/6/60, Edge Hill 3/61.

46244 Carlisle Upperby 14/6/58, Carlisle Kingmoor 3/61.

46245 Willesden 7/9/63, Crewe North 7/64.

46247 Carlisle Kingmoor 6/61. Some (probably best ignored) doubt as to allocation from 2/12/62 due to note on Card "NW 2/12/62". Loco photographed at probable home shed Carlisle Kingmoor immediately after official withdrawal W/E 25/5/63.

46251 something of a 'rogue', for it had by far the most individual allocations; maybe it used to balance up power requirements put out of kilter by works calls?

46252 Carlisle Upperby 11/6/61, Carlisle Kingmoor 3/61, Camden 22/9/62.

46255 Carlisle Upperby 26/6/48, Camden 6/52, Crewe North 20/9/52, Carlisle Upperby 25/2/56, Carlisle Kingmoor 3/61.

46256 whatever the reason for the 'same date' notation on on 7 and 21/11/59, allocation from 21/11/59 was definitely Carlisle Upperby.

46257 Carlisle Upperby 27/9/58, Carlisle Kingmoor 3/61.

points to the curiously muted beginnings of the Coronation Pacifics (or 'Princess Coronations' as they were at first awkwardly called): *The 1937 Building Programme listed 4F 0-6-0s, 3P 2-6-2Ts and diesel shunters, and was agreed on 26 July 1936. Normally such proposals went forward to the Board for 'rubber-stamping'. Now, the first five Coronation Pacifics, 6220-6224, were built in 1937 but authority only seems to have been given at a late stage, after the 1937 Programme got to the Board. Five more Princesses had been envisaged, but memories of West Coast - East Coast speed rivalry were being thoroughly stirred and a series of high speed tests conducted during 1936 proved that better timings on the West Coast were perfectly possible. A degree of secrecy, or at least discretion, was obviously thought prudent. Gresley's three week-old SILVER LINK had reached 112½mph (twice within ten minutes!) in September 1935, and SILVER FOX 113mph in 1936. The LMS effort was now only a matter of time, and the means to do it would be a class of 'improved Princesses'.* The Coronations were built over a protracted period in several batches:

1937: 6220-6224
6220 CORONATION
6221 QUEEN ELIZABETH
6222 QUEEN MARY
6223 PRINCESS ALICE
6224 PRINCESS ALEXANDRA
All streamlined

1938: 6225-6234
6225 DUCHESS OF GLOUCESTER
6226 DUCHESS OF NORFOLK
6227 DUCHESS OF DEVONSHIRE
6228 DUCHESS OF RUTLAND
6229 DUCHESS OF HAMILTON
All streamlined

6230 DUCHESS OF BUCCLEUCH
6231 DUCHESS OF ATHOLL
6232 DUCHESS OF MONTROSE
6233 DUCHESS OF SUTHERLAND
6234 DUCHESS OF ABERCORN
All non-streamlined

1939: 6235-6239
6235 CITY OF BIRMINGHAM
6236 CITY OF BRADFORD
6237 CITY OF BRISTOL
6238 CITY OF CARLISLE
6239 CITY OF CHESTER
All streamlined

1940: 6240-6244
6240 CITY OF COVENTRY
6241 CITY OF EDINBURGH
6242 CITY OF GLASGOW
6243 CITY OF LANCASTER
6244 CITY OF LEEDS (renamed KING GEORGE VI April 1941)
All streamlined

1943: 6245-6248
6245 CITY OF LONDON
6246 CITY OF MANCHESTER
6247 CITY OF LIVERPOOL
6248 CITY OF LEEDS
All streamlined

1944: 6249-6252
6249 CITY OF SHEFFIELD
6250 CITY OF LICHFIELD
6251 CITY OF NOTTINGHAM
6252 CITY OF LEICESTER
All non-streamlined

1946-48: 6253-6257
6253 CITY OF ST ALBANS
6254 CITY OF STOKE-ON-TRENT
6255 CITY OF HEREFORD
6256 SIR WILLIAM A. STANIER, F.R.S.
6257 CITY OF SALFORD
All non-streamlined

An 'official' to illustrate some of the features of the streamliners, though this is one of the famous 'fakes' – check the lists and you'll find CITY OF SHEFFIELD was 6249... The LMS, somewhat tiresomely, often swopped identities rather than haul out each locomotive in turn–far better to do a job lot simply by altering plates and numbers without the photographer having to lug his kit backwards and forwards! 'There's many a slip', however, and inevitably locos got out of sequence, minds were changed, and so on. See page 18 in *The Book of the Coronation Pacifics* for yet another of the fakes. It is said the pictures were taken to present to local dignitaries at naming ceremonies – no one then had our later-day angst concerning numbers! Despite the subterfuge, this picture shows well some of the typical features, especially the hollow axles and the motion. There was a concerted drive to reduce weight in the designing of the new Pacifics; something called 'Vibrac' steel was used for the motion and the fluted sections never gave the sort of problems later experienced on many types, most notably, perhaps, the BR Standards. The new steel was stronger and lighter than the manganese-molybdenum used in the Princess Pacifics and though at 11ft the connecting rods were 2ft longer than those on the Princesses, the new rods were 7lb lighter. Note also the lightweight front step, the ventilating louvres behind the buffers (the first batch of five did not have these), the sandbox fillers (the rear driver did not have sanding, it will be seen), position of workplate, the bracket for the Stone-Deuta 'speedo', the cowlings front and aft on the tender, the sliding door to get the 'bag' in when taking water and the holes in the casing around the firebox for the washout plugs.

4

That hybrid animal, the 'semi' 46245 CITY OF LONDON at Shrewsbury; behind is one of the Westinghouse-fitted Britannias, either 70043 or 70044 which carried the gear between 1952 and 1955. The Britannia would be at Shrewsbury after a visit to Crewe; the 'big 'un' is not in particularly sparkling condition so is likely to be on one of those fill-in runs in between work on the West Coast route. The Transport Treasury.

A Coronation in final condition: CITY OF LONDON at Old Oak Common, 1 September 1964 in a series of photographs to show all the Coronation detail as it was at the last. She was to work an Ian Allan railtour from Paddington that day, and was prepared by an Old Oak Driver and Fireman, as depicted in several of the photographs. Coronation visits to Euston had become fewer and farther between that year and this was considered to be the very last time in the capital for a Stanier Pacific. They had been banned south of Crewe under the 25kV of course since the beginning of September, hence the yellow stripe on the cab side. I took these both to record the last visit (remember they helped out during the 'King Withdrawal Crisis' some years previously) as well as some detail for the modeller i.e. their final condition. This is the traditional three-quarter front view – note recessed handholds on the smoke deflectors. Screw coupling 'hooked up' out of the way. Correct tail light for the light engine movement up to Paddington. Notes and photograph (courtesy The Transport Treasury) by Alec Swain – who worked there at the time.

Front end detail. AWS receiver with protective shield prominent. Cut-away valancing to show easy access for piston valve removal when necessary. The top lamp iron on many LMR locomotives was lowered to the smokebox door in these years – for laudable reasons – but it was aesthetically displeasing. The Coronations hardly suffered this – though take a look at 46255 in *Accompaniment:2*, page 44... Engine shed signal box just visible. Notes and photograph (courtesy The Transport Treasury) by Alec Swain.

CITY OF LONDON had long been one of Camden's finest and had come to Willesden with the rest a year or so before. By this time she was actually a Crewe North engine. Did she work 'special leave' up to London on the LNW line, despite the cabside stripe and the ban south of Crewe? Topping up the tender before leaving, the Fireman is holding the chain ready to swing the pipe round. Plenty of coal! Steam operated coal pusher to the left of the Fireman, who is about to descend; he will close the hatch over the filling point as he climbs down. Lamp to denote 'light engine' and a distant Hymek subsequently largely obscured by steam. Notes and photograph (courtesy The Transport Treasury) by Alec Swain.

Left. The Old Oak Driver and Fireman (pity I no longer have their names–will a reader write?). Maroon livery of course, marred by the hideous yellow stripe bounded by the lining. The slotted holder below the Driver's hand was for the short-lived driver nameplate. Nice under-the-cab details showing the live steam injector and footsteps on tender front. Note lining thereon.

Below. Had to include the GWR signal at the shed exit! Dismantled platelayers' trolley in foreground. Behind that concrete wall in the background is the Grand Union Canal. Note white-painted point levers which reduced the chance of blokes tripping over them in darkness/fog, though there was yard lighting (just visible in several of the photos). Notes and photographs (courtesy The Transport Treasury) by Alec Swain.

Above. Looking back towards the Factory (the Old Oak Repair Shop soon to be converted for diesels). Shows detail of the combined water feed valve and strainer between the wheels. The sieves within could be withdrawn and cleaned easily, once a stop valve had been closed. Many earlier locos had the sieves *inside* the tender water space and somebody (inevitably an apprentice) had to crawl inside to clean it out–ugh! Note detail of lining on tender frames. Notes and photograph (courtesy The Transport Treasury) by Alec Swain.

Left. Looking down towards the front of the shed and the Factory again. Speedometer drive off trailing crank pin. 94XX pannier just visible. Notes and photograph (courtesy The Transport Treasury) by Alec Swain.

More of those wonderful rivets. The square brass plate (it shows as white) on the truck frame records some experimental fitting which required notes and/or a regular report/examination. Notes and photograph (courtesy The Transport Treasury) by Alec Swain.

Almost up under CITY OF LONDON. Note detail of cylinder drain cocks, riveting, plating, bolts and all the rest. The bolted plate on the cylinder cover gave access to oil pipes within. This ends the close-up sequence of CITY OF LONDON. Notes and photograph (courtesy The Transport Treasury) by Alec Swain.

But we have some more detail here in a wonderful close-up of sand fillers, lubricators with the curious notch so that the lids could be fully opened and of course the motion and sand pipes. This is CITY OF BIRMINGHAM (note coat of arms) in its earlier life as a 'semi'. The good view of the brakes is interesting; they were 'articulated' with two blocks on a single hanger and a number of Stanier engines had such an arrangement. They never wore evenly and fitters always replaced the top one by the bottom one and put a new one on the bottom at brake block changes.

Left. View at Willesden shed from the cab of a Coronation in the 1960s, showing how it opened inward for cleaning. You wouldn't think that boiler handrail curved so much... Photograph J.G. Walmsley, The Transport Treasury.

Below. Works grey again – it certainly showed up the detail in photographs, which was the point after all. DUCHESS OF GLOUCESTER awaits its red and gold which, though probably the most magnificent livery devised by man, would tend to obscure the fine detail. Moreover the wheels and motion are also specially picked out in white. The 'speed whiskers' are a stroke of genius and you can just imagine a Robert Donat type character struggling with a villain in the cab as DUCHESS OF GLOUCESTER hurtles through the London suburbs, followed by a King at Slough and an A3 on the Forth Bridge until our hero finally alights at Lime Street from a Jubilee. Our DUCHESS was new in May 1938 and only two or three weeks later, in that sumptuous and shimmering red and gold, was selected to put on a bit of a show for German State Railway officers, travelling from Euston to Glasgow for a meeting of the Institution of Locomotive Engineers. And that's where Robert Donat might have come in again...

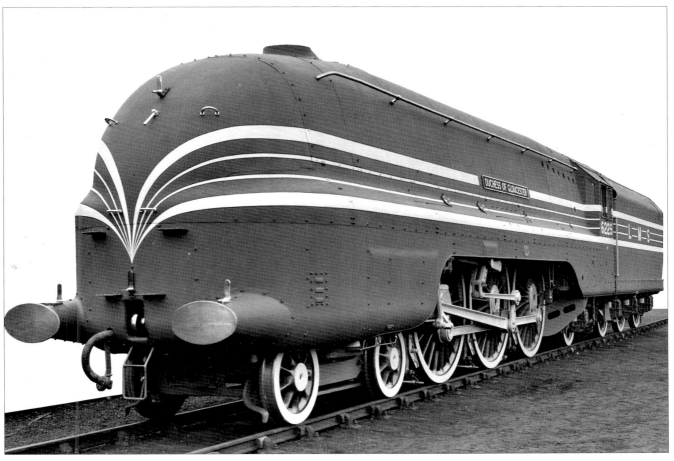

Left and opposite. If 100,000 miles a year could ever be attained it would be accomplished on the quality of the bearings. At least two firms were involved, Timken and SKF, with both claiming SIR WILLIAM as their own. The leading and trailing intermediate axles had Timken bearings in cannonboxes. This was not possible of course for the crank axle and Timken did not, apparently, make a suitable bearing. Hence SKF. The inset (a big end not an axle bearing) records a routine over-heating incident on one of the earlier engines, on this occasion with 46239 CITY OF CHESTER, when a 2-6-0 and CORONATION came to the rescue. The train was eventually 43 minutes late at Euston.

BR. RAILWAYS **MISHAP** G. H. Baker Esq. BR.30247

| DATE OF INCIDENT | 31.12.58. | TELEPHONE REPORT RECEIVED FROM | Crewe. |
| | | TIME RECEIVED | 3.0 p.m. |

Time of Incident 11.30 a.m. At Carnforth.

Train 8.30am Class 'A' Engine No. 46239 No. of Vehicles

From Glasgow. To Euston.

Driver Of

Guard Of

Shunter Of

Nature Engine failed with right hand big end hot.

Cause

Lines Affected Up main.

Single Line Working Between and

At

Normal Working Resumed at 11.38 a.m.

REMARKS : Engine No.2968 worked train forward at 11.38am and on arrival Lancaster driver requested fresh engine from Crewe. Train arrived Crewe.1.26 and left at 1.36 hauled by engine No.46220.

SKF
AT THE MOST
CRITICAL POSITIONS

ROLLER BEARINGS
FOR LOCOMOTIVE
INTERNAL - CRANK AXLES

THE internal-crank axle of the 4-6-2 locomotive "Sir William A. Stanier, F.R.S.", recently commissioned, is equipped with SKF Self-Aligning Spherical Roller Bearing Axleboxes. These bearings are the most suitable roller bearings which could be used in the confined space and give the required load capacity. They also provide the self-alignment necessary in view of axle flexures under load.

A further locomotive similarly equipped will shortly be commissioned.

THE SKEFKO BALL
BEARING CO., LTD.
LUTON

The
BRITISH MANUFACTURERS
OF THE WORLD RENOWNED
SKF BEARINGS

[To face first tex

The celebrated 'nose', a somewhat ponderous look to the modern eye perhaps. It was definitely a stirring sight at the time, however, especially with the stripes and the striking blue and red liveries. It had to be kept clean if it was not to look awful though, and the engines became thoroughly woebegone in the War, when cleaning was ignored for long periods. Note how the drawhook is secreted away, and just how precarious a position the Fireman had to get himself in, in order to put the top lamp in place. 'It wouldn't be allowed today!'

The footplate – it will never be this clean again. From left to right below the buffer beam are: the overflow from the live steam injector, water hose connection to live steam injector, carriage warming apparatus hose, steam brake pipe to tender, steam supply to the coal pusher on tender, water hose connection to the exhaust steam injector and the overflow from the exhaust steam injector. The drawbars sit within that elongated slot. The tender fall plate is in three sections which catered for track irregularities, not least when trundling around in shed yards. The speedometer dial is fitted just above the left-hand cab front window, with vacuum train pipe gauge to the right and above. There is a backing plate for a steam chest pressure gauge, which does not seem to have ever been fitted, in the event. On the Fireman's side is the boiler pressure gauge (large) and smaller 'steam heat' (carriage warming) pressure gauge. The 'sand gun' sits just above the firehole doors – it directed a jet of sand under steam pressure to clear the tubes but was later removed as ineffective. The sliding roof ventilator has been opened, to illuminate the cab for the photograph.

The tender rear, illustrating the features unique to the streamlined engines; this is tender No.9745 which was first fitted to 6227 DUCHESS OF DEVONSHIRE. Note the extended fairing, the water fillers at each side (each of which had to be accessed through a sliding hatch) and the ladder. The apparatus with the pipes over the dome is the coal pusher provided for all the engines, streamlined or conventional and the oiling points are neatly marked in white (this soon disappeared).

Engine Picking the Coronations
A Brief Guide

And brief it must be, for variation and change was enormous within the class. This should at least whet the reader's appetite for the more lengthy and detailed account in *The Book of the Coronation Pacifics*. As remarked in that book, there can hardly be more fertile ground for the 'engine picker'—that devotee of detail—than the Coronation Pacifics. For a start (apart from half-hearted experiment with single locos) the class could not have enjoyed any difference more fundamental than its division, unique in British practice, into streamlined and non-streamlined forms. Moreover the unconscionable time taken to complete what was a relatively small class, together with the 'de-streamlining' process, exaggerated the range of detail variation. As remarked before: *Some engines were losing the streamlined casing before some of the later 'conventionals' appeared new from Crewe!*

The Streamlining Goes. The three tons of streamlining case (it looks somewhat less than dashing to the modern eye) was attached to a framework of light steel, the whole making for some devilishly awkward maintenance. Worse, it offered nothing in terms of extra performance. The crunch came with the War and it was Ivatt, in 1945, that ordered it finally done away with.

Smokeboxes. So it was that 6235 CITY OF BIRMINGHAM was the first streamliner to become 'conventional', in April 1946. Thus was born a further set of detail differences different again from those Coronations built non-streamlined from the first. The most peculiar of these was the sloping smokebox top – hence the epithet 'semi'. There was no reason, of course, to discard a perfectly serviceable smokebox and so the sloping topped ones were retained until they were condemned in the normal course of things. It was 1952 before the engines started getting new smokeboxes to the conventional pattern and the last was not done, incredibly, until 1960!

Front Framing. Removal of the casing left a more 'utilitarian' front end, with no curved plating in front of the cylinders, which was of course useful for maintenance. New engines from 6253 to 6257 were similar. Oddly the engines that were built 'conventional' from the first, 6230-6234 and 6249-6252 kept the footplate draped in front of the cylinders, so perhaps its absence wasn't so useful after all. The Harrow disaster engine, 46242, had been 'de-streamlined' in March 1947 and its replacement (a new engine not a repair, we all suspect) emerged from Crewe with the original footplating duly curving down in front of its cylinders, in proper 1930s fashion.

We have seen enough of CORONATION in original streamlined guise in earlier pages – this is how the 'stirring spectacle' of June 1937 that touched 114mph looked after conversion, running as a 'semi' (somewhere near Shap by the look of it) about 1953. It did not get a replacement smokebox until 1955. The name, it is worth noting, marked King George VI's Coronation of 1937; the next four of the 1937 batch were all named after the immediate Royal Family, the Queen, the Queen Mother and two Princesses who had not had a Princess Royal Pacific named after them.

SOME DETAILS

Loco	To traffic	S/C	Tender No.	DC	SD added	SB restored
46220	6/37	S	9703	12/44	9/46	12/55
46221	6/37	S	9704	11/40	5/46	9/52
46222	6/37	S	9705	8/43	5/46	8/53
46223	7/37	S	9706	11/41	8/46	8/55
46224	7/37	S	9707	5/40	5/46	10/54
46225	5/38	S	9743	6/43	2/47	1/55
46226	5/38	S	9744	7/42	6/47	11/55
46227	6/38	S	9745	12/40	2/47	5/53
46228	6/38	S	9746	9/40	7/47	1/57
46229	9/38	S	9747	4/43	11/47	2/57
46230	6/38	C	9748	10/40	9/46	-
46231	6/38	C	9749	6/40	9/46	-
46232	7/38	C	9750	1/43	2/45	-
46233	7/38	C	9751	3/41	9/46	-
46234	8/38	C	9752	2/39	3/46	-
46235	7/39	S	9798	New	4/46	7/52
46236	7/39	S	9799	New	12/47	11/53
46237	8/39	S	9800	New	1/47	5/56
46238	9/39	S	9801	New	11/46	10/53
46239	9/39	S	9802	New	6/47	2/57
46240	3/40	S	9803	New	6/47	5/57
46241	4/40	S	9804	New	1/47	2/58
46242	5/40	S	9805	New	3/47	11/53
46243	6/40	S	9806	New	5/49	11/58
46244	7/40	S	9807	New	8/47	7/53
46245	6/43	S	9808	New	8/47	12/57
46246	8/43	S	9809	New	9/46	5/60
46247	9/43	S	9810	New	5/47	5/58
46248	10/43	S	9811	New	12/46	6/58
46249	4/44	C	9812	New	11/46	-
46250	5/44	C	9813	New	3/46	-
46251	6/44	C	9814	New	8/46	-
46252	6/44	C	9815	New	3/45	
46253	9/46	C	9816	New	New	-
46254	9/46	C	9817	New	New	-
46255	10/46	C	10622	New	New	-
46256	12/47	C	10623	New	New	-
46257	5/48	C	10624	New	New	-

S = Streamliner
C = Conventional
SD = Smoke Deflector
SB = Smokebox
DC = Double Chimney

Smoke Deflectors. The distinctive and handsome deflectors first appeared on 6232 and 6252 in 1945 with the rest of the non-streamliners following the next year. The 'de-streamlined' ones got the deflectors when they lost their casings. The job cost £45, which must make the preservationists sigh for the good old days.

Double Chimney. A double blastpipe and chimney on the other hand, cost about £70. The alteration had first taken place, experimentally, on 6234 DUCHESS OF ABERCORN; all subsequent engines got the double chimney and earlier ones were modified when next in works. Allen (*British Pacific Locomotives*, Ian Allan, 1962) makes the point that the double

chimney as fitted to the class as a whole was *not* a Kylchap arrangement. The Kylchap on the LNER was a series of petticoats, one below the other between the base of the chimney and the blast orifices. The arrangement on the Coronations was simpler, the blastpipe branching into two with the two chimneys, in line, sited above. These variations are best summarised in the table above.

Speed Indicators. A form of 'speedo', mounted on a cumbersome hanging bracket, appeared on 6220-6224 and others, too, apparently. Before the War these 'speed indicators' were to be widely fitted to nearly a thousand locos but this never materialised. In January 1947 rather less than half that number were ordered so fitted but this too came

to nought. It was in fact the late 1950s before the familiar BR 'speedo', driven off the left-hand trailing crank pin, became universal, though 46256 and 46257 apparently were equipped from new.

Cab Windows
Larger cab front windows were required for the 'de-streamlined' engines.

Tenders
Ten ton welded tenders with steam operated coal pushers were provided for the Coronations. The streamlined ones had the side sheets extended back to close the gap between the rear of the tender and the front of the first coach, in a rather doomed attempt, you suspect, to smooth the airflow of the 'streamlined' train. Sliding doors in the top of this fairing either side allowed access for the water column hoses. There was also a cowl at the front, matching the outline of the cab roof, though at first those on the 1937 batch, 6220-6224, did not have this. The tenders of the conventional engines, of course, had none of these features. Welding was later abandoned and the last five post-War engines had distinctive riveting. Non-streamlined tenders on 6249-6252 went into traffic 'partially streamlined' having already been built in anticipation of more streamlined locomotives. They were duly modified. The rear sheets on the streamlined tenders began to disappear in the War years to make access easier and once an engine was 'de-streamlined' all tenders looked more or less the same, apart from at the front, where it met the cab. As *The Book of the Coronation Pacifics* puts it: *On most the tender front was cut away high up, matching the inward curve of the tender tops. This was the case with all the streamlined engines and the later conventional ones but the first conventional batch, 6230-6234, had a lower 'sweep', and so did the last two, 6256 and 46257. Former streamlined tenders were recognisable by the vestigial sheeting at the rear, extending back by an inch or two, and the access ladder.*

A table in the excellent *An Illustrated History of LMS Locomotives Volume 5* (Essery and Jenkinson, Silver Link, 1989) gives the disposition of the tenders on the class as built. I've taken the liberty of adapting and extracting a portion thereof:
First conventional batch 6230-6234 = non-streamlined, welded tank, low front cutaway.
Conventional batch 1946 6253-6255 = non-streamlined, riveted tank, high front cutaway.
Last two 6256 and 46257 = non-streamlined, riveted tank, low front cutaway.
All the rest = streamlined, welded tank, high front cutaway.

Liveries. Now it really gets complicated – as J.P. Rowledge has put it, of *eleven* liveries used only one—BR lined green, from August 1955 to December 1957—applied to the whole class at the same time! A table summarises the story best (right).

The Last Two: Rocking Grates, Roller Bearings and 100,000 Miles a Year

The final major difference came with the last pair of Coronations of 1947-48. They were built (at least in part) to compare steam with Ivatt's new diesel 'Twins', 10000 and 10001. With roller bearings, rocking grates, self cleaning smokebox and hopper ashpan it was hoped to push mileages to 100,000 per year, extend shopping periods and cut time on shed. The trailing trucks on these last two were very different and the whole rear end was redesigned. The old framing was replaced by a sort of bar frame extension; the new Delta truck looked very different and meant that the cab sides could be reduced, losing the attractive curved bottom to the cab.

AWS/ATC. A prominent feature (or rather the shield protecting the front screw coupling was) there were also vacuum reservoirs and battery box on the running plate. AWS appeared only late and some examples carried it for only three years or so.

LIVERY CHANGES

No	First Livery	War. black	Exp. grey	LMS black	BR black	BR blue	BR green	BR red
6220	Blue	3/44	-	10/46	-	1/50	8/52	-
6221	Blue	8/44	-	7/46	-	2/50*	1/52	-
6222	Blue	10/44	-	5/46	-	9/50*	12/52	-
6223	Blue	2/44	-	8/46	-	3/50	9/52	-
6224	Blue	10/44	-	7/46	-	5/48#	4/52	-
6225	Red	4/44	-	3/47	-	2/50	2/53	8/58
6226	Red	?/44	-	6/47	11/48	5/49	4/51*	11/58
6227	Red	1/44	-	3/47	-	5/48#	5/53	-
6228	Red	4/44	-	11/47	-	8/50	8/55	6/58
6229	Red	8/43*	-	12/47	-	1/50*	3/52	9/58
6230	Red	-	-	9/46	-	5/48#	3/52	-
6231	Red	8/45*	-	9/46	-	5/48#	11/53	-
6232	Red	2/45	-	9/47	-	-	11/51*	-
6233	Red	-	-	9/46	-	-	12/52*	-
6234	Red	-	3/46	-	-	5/48#	1/52	-
6235	Red	3/43	-	4/46	-	10/50*	4/53	-
6236	Red	4/44	-	12/47	-	-	8/55	7/58
6237	Red	8/43*	-	2/47	-	8/49*	8/52*	-
6238	Red	?/43	-	8/46	3/49	-	10/53	6/58
6239	Red	3/44*	-	9/47	-	6/50*	7/54*	-
6240	Red	11/45	-	7/47	-	1/50	9/54*	7/58
6241	Red	5/43*	-	2/47	-	5/48#	4/53*	-
6242	Red	5/44	-	5/47	-	8/49	11/53	-
6243	Red	1/44	-	-	-	6/49	1/54*	10/58
6244	Red	1/44	-	8/47	-	9/48#	5/53	10/58
6245	Black	New	-	11/47	-	-	4/53	12/57
6246	Black	New	-	11/46	11/48	-	5/53*	10/58
6247	Black	New	-	2/47	-	-	1/54*	5/58
6248	Black	New	-	1/47	3/49	-	8/53*	6/58
6249	Black	New	-	11/46	-	8/50*	1/53*	-
6250	Black	New	-	7/47	-	3/50*	9/52*	-
6251	Black	New	-	6/47	4/49	-	10/51*	11/58
6252	Black	New	-	11/46*	3/49	?/50	1/54*	-
6253	Black	-	-	New	-	-	10/53*	-
6254	Black	-	-	New	-	8/50*	1/53**	9/58
6255	Black	-	-	New	-	6/50	4/53	-
6256	Black	-	-	New	11/48	3/51*	5/54*	5/58
6257	Black	-	-	-	New	-	11/52*	-

*Table adapted from Rowledge (*The LMS Pacifics, *D&C 1987*), with kind permission.*
*approximate—probably into service some weeks later
#'experimental' blue when first painted
**This date appeared in 'The Book Of' and in the British Railways Illustrated Coronation Special of August 2001. Graham Onley's fading memories, bolstered by recent correspondence in the railway press, suggest 46254 retained blue until 1954...
46236, 46256 and 46257 ran with tenders lettered BRITISH RAILWAYS

CORONATION in a highly unusual setting – the ex-GW St Philip's Marsh shed in Bristol on 8 February 1963. It had worked in unexpectedly (to say the least) with a parcels from Crewe via Hereford and the Severn Tunnel. Coronations were not authorised to run this route and it had to be returned far more expeditiously... CORONATION had an odd history of course, for it spent the years immediately before and during much of the War impersonating 6229 DUCHESS OF HAMILTON which had gone to the United States got up as CORONATION. Photograph Terry Nicholls.

6221 QUEEN ELIZABETH in blue. The Art Deco 'winged' lamps are noteworthy (if one survives somewhere, tell me!) but the fully inspired effect of the 'speed whiskers' is ruined by the pasted train indication 'W27'. Note also drawhook in its recess and the flimsy front footsteps; also the cab window, markedly different in size from 'de-streamlined' or non-streamlined engines. The 'speedo' with its rearwards horizontal driving spindle was unique to the first five locos. Photograph Gavin Whitelaw Collection.

46221 QUEEN ELIZABETH making a tremendous show as it passes its home shed, Polmadie. With this level of cleanliness and the locals all agog, it would seem someone special was on board – a princess at the least, or maybe the PM? Photograph J. Robertson, The Transport Treasury.

Streamlined 6222 QUEEN MARY hurries through an empty Tamworth in the late 1930s. It must have been doubly frustrating for Stanier to have the streamlining forced upon him, for weight *reduction* was regarded as vital to the design. Yet despite the casing and its supporting framing, more than five tons had been saved; just as well, for the locomotives were right up to the Civil Engineer's limit. *The Railway Gazette* reported that without this five ton saving, brought about by modern materials and techniques, the boiler and therefore the output of the locomotive would have been considerably reduced. We should try to appreciate now the sense of wonder that greeted the streamlined trains and locomotives in the 1930s, reviving as they did the rivalries of the great 'Races to the North', which still lingered in living memory. Photograph The Transport Treasury.

Remarkable view of Camden bank as 46222 QUEEN MARY blasts northwards past Camden shed and the staff footbridge. Just marvel at the coaches, disappearing down the incline.

Clearly undeterred by posts, the photographer couldn't resist a pair of 'big 'uns' at Polmadie, 28 August 1961. At the front is 46222 QUEEN MARY and behind, 46231 DUCHESS OF ATHOLL. For long periods the Polmadie engine hauling the Royal Scot came off at Carlisle where it was replaced by a Camden one. The Polmadie engine returned to Glasgow with the down working, a practice which meant, over time, that the Polmadie 'big 'uns' accumulated lower mileages than their Crewe and Camden sisters. It was the desire to increase mileages that brought Polmadie Coronations through to London on this train during some summers. See the next *Accompaniment* for more of this sort of thing. The Coronations at Polmadie were there really for political reasons and it is significant that when the LMR got its EE Type 4 fleet up and running Polmadie was excluded. Photograph K.C.H. Fairey.

46223 PRINCESS ALICE was another Polmadie stalwart, spending the great part of her working life there. So while she'll get the spotters cheering at Euston later in the day, it was out of the ordinary (almost) at Glasgow Central if she *didn't* put in an appearance. Here she is on 9 June 1956 with the Royal Scot – the horizontal ROYAL SCOT headboard is interesting; as pointed out in *The Book of the Coronation Pacifics*, it seems to have been introduced in June 1950 (without the tartan) for the diesel 'Twins' 10000-10001 and the Southern trio 10201-10203. The traditional curved headboard remained in use for steam locomotives. Photograph J. Robertson, The Transport Treasury.

46224 PRINCESS ALEXANDRA from an unusual viewpoint, with the pit deliberately illuminated for the photograph. This was the third of that first batch of 1937 to spend more or less its entire working life at Polmadie. The picture is not dated but would be some time between 'de-streamlining' in June 1946 and the fitting of a conventional smokebox towards the end of 1954 (for a sight of her looking extremely woebegone at the end of her streamlined career see page 21 in *The Book of the Coronation Pacifics*). The location would be the Repair Shop at Polmadie; the angle makes the sloping smokebox look odder still but we have a good view of the GW-type de Glehn bogie for once.

46224 PRINCESS ALEXANDRA at Kingmoor by the look of it, again from an unusual angle, the deep shadows emphasising that monstrous bulk. It has AWS and the electrification flashes so the period would be early 1960s. There are two firebox failures with fatal consequences recorded for the Coronations; both, astonishingly, befell the same locomotive, PRINCESS ALEXANDRA. The first killed the hapless Fireman on the climb to Craigenhill on 10 September 1940 and the second took the life of the Driver on 5 March 1948, at Lamington a mere twelve miles away... Photograph B. Richardson, The Transport Treasury.

46225 DUCHESS OF GLOUCESTER comes into Glasgow Central with the 11.20am from Birmingham on 23 April 1959. As noted in *The Book of the Coronation Pacifics*, 6225 (as a streamliner) was the train engine in one of the nastier accidents that involved Coronations. This was the derailed 'Services sleeper' at Mossband on 15 May 1944, when three passengers were killed. 46225 is also notable for being the Coronation tested at the Rugby Plant in the 1950s; it generated such power that the ensuing Report concluded that the locomotives were really working within the capabilities of the single Fireman, rather than the boiler... Photograph W.A.C. Smith.

A maroon 46226 DUCHESS OF NORFOLK, work-stained but with that look of enormous power waiting to burst forth that characterised the engines, at Carlisle on 27 May 1959. With a full tender she will be off south after attaching that coach to its next train – a single vehicle which only serves to increase the impression of bulk and purpose. Like one or two others, it got the style of BR lining which went with the green engines, and very good such examples looked, too. It was very quickly eradicated but was at least as attractive as the (in effect) 'LMS' lining of the maroon engines. Photograph R.C. Riley, The Transport Treasury.

46227 DUCHESS OF DEVONSHIRE, with the first emblem on the tender, at some anonymous point on the LM. It settled on Polmadie in 1948 after moving round Crewe, Camden and Carlisle and stayed there through BR days. Photograph The Transport Treasury.

46228 DUCHESS OF RUTLAND, equipped with AWS, electrification flashes while on the other side there will be a 'speedo' too. The loco sits on one of the Crewe North turntable stalls in April 1964; withdrawal was only a few months away. Alongside is Black Five 44761 and, on the right, Britannia Pacific 70030 WILLIAM WORDSWORTH and one of the 'City' series of Coronations. Photograph D. Beecroft, The Transport Treasury.

46229 DUCHESS OF HAMILTON at Shrewsbury with another Camden example, 46254 CITY OF STOKE-ON-TRENT. Both are in shiny ex-works condition and as both left Crewe (newly red) in September 1958 this is presumably the year of this meeting, before despatch to Camden for regular work. 46254 was 'booked out' from a Light Intermediate on 8 September 1958 and 46229 two days later, after a Heavy Intermediate. We now have the prospect of the National Railway Museum returning DUCHESS OF HAMILTON to streamlined condition! Photograph The Transport Treasury.

A sad decline for DUCHESS OF HAMILTON, 24 September 1961, before its rescue by Sir Billy and installation at the Minehead camp. It had ended up as part of a small stud of 8P Pacifics at Edge Hill and though the London jobs were given over to EE Type 4 diesels, the Pacifics' principal role was to serve as replacements whenever the Type 4s failed. Three or four at times would be standing ready, fully coaled with steam up prepared for the call, which came all too frequently. Photograph K.C.H. Fairey.

A Polmadie engine through and through, 46230 DUCHESS OF BUCCLEUCH (its pronunciation quite defeated the lineside unwashed – in New Southgate anyway) stands at Platform 4 on a wet evening at Carlisle Citadel, 23 May 1960. The train is the 7.35pm semi-fast to Glasgow St Enoch; Newton Heath Jubilee 45642 BOSCAWEN stands adjacent with a Liverpool and Manchester train to Glasgow Central. Photograph W.A.C. Smith.

46230 DUCHESS OF BUCCLEUCH going off its home shed Polmadie, 24 June 1960. In this light the hollow axles and 'Vibrac' steel motion show up well and sharply. These are features owed to the drive for weight reduction – that famous five and a bit tons. Stronger and lighter than the manganese-molybdenum used in the Princess Pacifics, the 'Vibrac' connecting rods were 2ft longer but 7lb lighter than those on the Princesses. Such is the measure of progress. Photograph W.A.C. Smith.

A fine portrait of 46231 DUCHESS OF ATHOLL at its Polmadie home, in beautiful late light at the front of the grand old shed on 22 August 1953. Photograph James Stevenson, courtesy Hamish Stevenson.

46232 DUCHESS OF MONTROSE near Shrewsbury, possibly in 1960 after its last Heavy General, in the autumn of 1960. It is engaged on one of those 'trial trips', coupled to other newly-overhauled engines – in this case a Jubilee and a 2-6-4T. Photograph The Transport Treasury.

46233 DUCHESS OF SUTHERLAND, another with a fine Scottish name which never worked from Polmadie, leaving Birmingham New Street, Platform 3, 24 March 1962 with the 4.2pm Wolverhampton High Level-Euston. Behind is a Birmingham RCW DMU on a local service. Photograph Michael Mensing.

46233 DUCHESS OF SUTHERLAND at Willesden on 4 June 1963. The rambling old freight shed by the canal proved an unexpected home for all manner of Pacifics after Camden went over to diesels in 1962. It not only gained its own stud but also, perforce, serviced any others working in, such as Edge Hill's DUCHESS OF SUTHERLAND, later to be preserved via Butlin's, Ayr. For a period Willesden was a mesmerising place, a sort of Crewe North and Crewe South combined. As has been noted wistfully in these columns, both in *The Book(s) of the Coronation Pacifics* and *British Railways Illustrated*, the RCTS recorded that on 5 July 1964 no less than *seven* Coronations were on shed there: 'probably the maximum present here at any one time, being 46225(12B), 46238(12B), 46239(1A), 46240(1A), 46241(8A), 46245(1A) and 46248(5A), with 46240 and 46245 in their accustomed immaculate condition'. This was not the end of it, for as well as the Stanier Pacifics two Royal Scots had turned up that day and there were eight Jubilees and another *eight* Britannias. Photograph Peter Groom.

46234 DUCHESS OF ABERCORN at Rugby, 1 September 1962. The engine was part of that first conventional batch and so has one of the tenders that never bore a hint of streamlining – hence the traditional vent pipes at the rear. Photograph The Transport Treasury.

46235 CITY OF BIRMINGHAM northbound through the closed Minshall Vernon (once the first station north of Crewe, before Winsford) in 1952, shortly before the smokebox was 'done'. Photograph P. Ward.

46241 CITY OF EDINBURGH, oddly never based in Scotland, at Shrewsbury shed on one of those turns from Crewe North. Photograph The Transport Treasury.

Front end contrast at Camden (there was never a blacker girder in Britain) on 5 June 1960, as 46242 CITY OF GLASGOW is readied for The Ulster Express. The locomotive had been 'renewed' after the Harrow collision of 1952. The fireman's job before moving off was to sweep the detritus of smokebox cleaning off the front, so it could not blow back during running. On a minor domestic note – observe the tea 'can' in the shed window. Photograph Peter Groom.

46243 CITY OF LANCASTER with another yet prodigious load, near Baswich, approaching Stafford from the south during 1962. Photograph P. Ward.

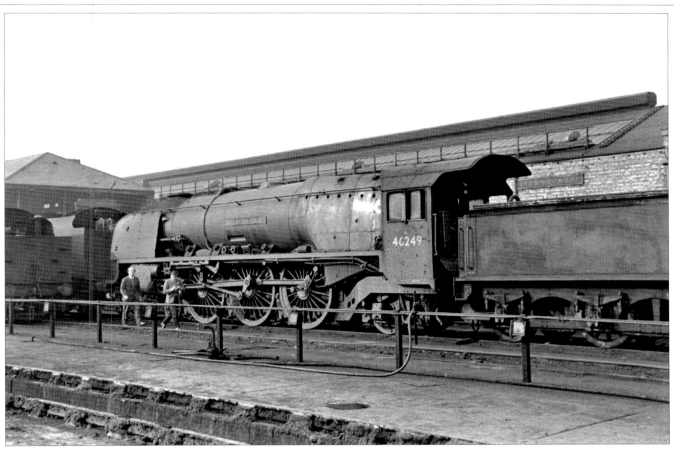

Every book needs a joke: awaiting entry to the works, CITY OF SHEFFIELD stands on the Steam Cleaning Pits at Crewe – the Iron Foundry forms the backdrop. Its own tender has already been whisked off and chance has seen it parked next to a tender from a Super D 0-8-0. Photograph B. Richardson, The Transport Treasury.

46250 CITY OF LICHFIELD, in late condition with AWS, at Crewe. The Pacifics were so big and so powerful that on some jobs they constantly threatened to run away from the best efforts of the Fireman. The great bulk plunging into certain single bore tunnels could force a momentary blow-back and crews learnt to retreat to the cab corners. It is hard to visualise how this would be incorporated into a safety manual today... Write to The Editor, *British Railways Illustrated,* 59A High Street, Clophill, Bedfordshire, MK45 4BE with your version of what it might be. We'll publish the funniest one and its creator will win the next 'Book Of'. Free! Photograph The Transport Treasury.

46251 CITY OF NOTTINGHAM, in black with straw BR numbers but still with LMS on the tender, takes a London-Glasgow train through Lichfield Trent Valley, Saturday 26 June 1948. Photograph F.W. Shuttleworth.

46252 CITY OF LEICESTER with the Mid-Day Scot at Beattock, 2 May 1953. Because it was built conventionally and so did not get 'de-streamlined' it has the sloping front to the footplating. The notch for the 'cleaner's toe cap' has yet to appear at the base of the smoke deflector. The engine spent more or less its entire working life shared between Camden and Crewe North with brief three month spells at Upperby until a two year stay at the Carlisle shed 1960-1962. Then it was back to Camden and 'normal service' was resumed. In some years it could be thus be one of those elusive nocturnal ones. Photograph J. Robertson, The Transport Treasury.

46252 CITY OF LEICESTER in traditional moorland setting, just beginning the descent to Tebay with the up Royal Scot; beyond the last coach to the right of the line is Shap Summit box with Shap Quarry opposite The carriage roof boards give the train away, with white lettering on a tartan background. These lasted from the early 1950s until fading away in the early 1960s. 46252 was condemned in June 1963 and the 'IM20' was introduced in 1961 which pins the period down a little.

46252 CITY OF LEICESTER with the Mid-Day Scot at Beattock, 2 May 1953. Because it was built conventionally and so did not get 'de-streamlined' it has the sloping front to the footplating. The notch for the 'cleaner's toe cap' has yet to appear at the base of the smoke deflector. The engine spent more or less its entire working life shared between Camden and Crewe North with brief three month spells at Upperby until a two year stay at the Carlisle shed 1960-1962. Then it was back to Camden and 'normal service' was resumed. In some years it could be thus be one of those elusive nocturnal ones. Photograph J. Robertson, The Transport Treasury.

46253 CITY OF ST ALBANS in the semi-roundhouse at Crewe North, 11 November 1962 after some last minute cleaning (note the rag on the connecting rod and the oil bottle on the floor). Malcolm the photographer observed this cleaning though you'd have to point out that, according to the Record Card, the engine was in store at this time. We'll never quite know *everything* will we?... The first of the trio of 1946, it was the first conventional one to have the 'utilitarian' front end (in which the running plate in front of the cylinders was dispensed with) after the fashion of the first 'de-streamlined' example, 6235 CITY OF BIRMINGHAM which had appeared in April 1946. The LMS concentrated the heavier Pacific valve and piston examinations at Crewe North, so that all of them came there for the 'No.8' at 30-36,000 miles. Other maintenance could be undertaken at the same time and repair work benefited from the proximity of Crewe Works. The work was done in the dead end Middle Shed, by a special gang of men under their own Foreman. From Nationalisation Regional sensitivities meant the Polmadie ones were dealt with on their home patch and Crewe North looked after the LM-based engines only. Photograph Malcolm S. Castledine.

An excellent demonstration of the functioning of the smoke deflectors, CITY OF ST ALBANS with the 1.5pm Euston-Perth/Blackpool approaching Lichfield on 3 March 1962. See also page 48 of *The Book of the Coronation Pacifics* for another dramatic illustration of this phenomenon. Photograph Michael Mensing.

Above. Truly a beauty; the last Coronation, 46257 CITY OF SALFORD at Kingmoor in LMS lined black, 25 May 1952. The last two for a few years had steam turbo generators for the electric lights – that's the apparatus for it behind the smoke deflector. Electric lights, except for the Bulleid Pacifics perhaps, were never a resounding success in Britain – fire irons carelessly wielded, the buffeting of coaling plants and a complete unfamiliarity at the sheds doomed them on BR; let's face it, it took years to abandon oil lamps even on *diesels*. Photograph The Transport Treasury.

Below. Working on a 'big 'un' at Rugby shed, 25 April 1962. SIR WILLIAM, a Crewe North stalwart, would have failed somewhat violently out on the line somewhere in service – the radius rod is twisted and broken and hanging down ahead of the reversing link. On the ground from left to right are the mortal remains of the combining lever, union link, the other half of the radius rod and the valve rod, followed by both outside piston valves, and the right-hand piston valve front cover. As Allan Baker described in *British Railways Illustrated* Vol.11 No.7 (April 2002): *The cover from the opposite side can also be seen on the floor,* underneath the left-hand front footstep. In front of the piston valve, on the right, is the union link bracket, which has been removed from the crosshead with the other bit of the union link still attached – clearly this component too, had been broken in half. On the framing, by the length of rope, can be seen the pin used to connect the rocker arm for actuating the inside right-hand valve from the right-hand side valve gear, to the valve rod, indicating that this component has been removed too. So what has befallen SIR WILLIAM? Well, one would have expected a seized piston valve, either inside or outside, to have precipitated this sort of damage, but the two outside valves on the 'deck' show no signs of seizure and why, one wonders, has the left-hand one been removed – is there significant damage on the other side of the engine too? Perhaps the rocker arm had seized, as it appears to have been removed, but I can never recall such an incident on one of these engines – and note that neither of the inside valves have been removed. Several of the removed bits are not in evidence, including the valve rod crossheads and indeed the rocker arm – doubtless the Fitters had gone to lunch! Whatever, the engine was repaired and went on to give a few more years service.* Photograph Jack Hodgkinson.

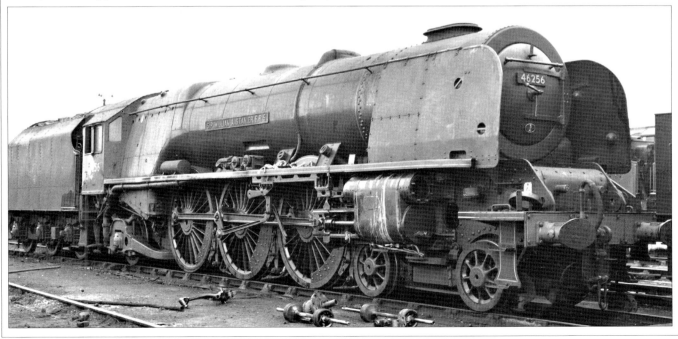

Truly a beauty; the last Coronation, 46257 CITY OF SALFORD at Kingmoor in LMS lined black, 25 May 1952. The last two for a few years had steam turbo generators for the electric lights – that's the apparatus for it behind the smoke deflector. Electric lights, except for the Bulleid Pacifics perhaps, were never a resounding success in Britain – fire irons carelessly wielded, the buffeting of coaling plants and a complete unfamiliarity at the sheds doomed them on BR; let's face it, it took years to abandon oil lamps even on *diesels*. Photograph The Transport Treasury.

A last look in the last of the light at Shrewsbury shed about 1962; the electric lighting is now gone but the uprights for the lamps (with conventional lamp irons alongside) are still there on the buffer beam. CITY OF SALFORD is blowing ready for the job ahead while the driver oils the little end – the oil bottle is on the ground by the middle driving wheel. The engine will be on one of those fill-in turns from her Carlisle Kingmoor home, out and back from Crewe before returning north with a train. Notice the 'Delta' trailing truck of the last two (thus the different cab profile) and the AWS battery box underneath. The tender leading axle box on the left-hand side has a curious projection, the mileage recorder; the last two, 46256 and 46257 had these and from examination of a number of photographs there was one each side. It can only mean that one read forward running and the other rearward running! Photograph Paul Chancellor Collection.

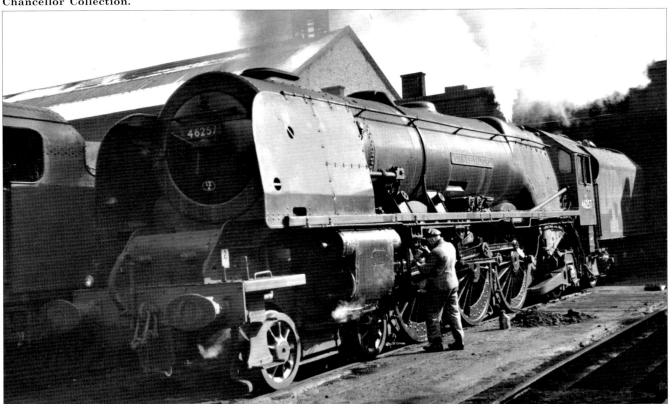